OUR CHRISTIAN JOURNEY

Jesus answered,"I am the way and the truth and the life.
No one come to the Father except through me."

For the newly introduced Christian

RUTH ROBAINE

authorHOUSE®

AuthorHouse™ UK Ltd.
500 Avebury Boulevard
Central Milton Keynes, MK9 2BE
www.authorhouse.co.uk
Phone: 08001974150

Editorial Coordination: Stephen Beitel

First published by AuthorHouse 10/20/2009

ISBN: 978-1-4389-7298-5 (sc)

This book is printed on acid-free paper.

The purpose of writing this book is to open the eyes of many people. I was motivated by my son's interest in the life of a Christian. As Mpho was growing up, he used to ask me many questions about Christian living, wanting so much to live to please God. When disciplining him, I would tell him that by doing what was not good, he was pleasing Satan. Knowing how much he dislikes Satan, it will make him stop immediately and ask forgiveness because God was his Hero and he didn't want to disappoint Him at all. So this inspired me to write for him that he can learn more as he grows up. I also engaged in many conversations with different people from different congregations claiming to be Christians. They believed that, as they were attending church on Sundays, that was enough for them to be called Christians. I could not blame them, because that was how they were led to believe.

They thought by doing that, their destiny would be heaven, and their ways were being prepared. I spoke to them about the Holy Spirit, to find out if they knew who He was, and what His purpose in the life of a Christian was. I was so disappointed to find out that most of them did not know much about Him and it gave me more courage to write this book, thinking about people who believe that they are saved and are not. I knew that it was not enough to only explain this to those I come to contact with, while many people claiming to be Christians believe in different things that are not according to Jesus' teachings.

The book of Matthew chapter 24 also inspired me, where it spoke about the Antichrists, which I couldn't understand at first, and then I prayed for God's revelation and also asked him to open my eyes for me not to be deceived by their appearance on earth when that time arrives. The more I was engaged in different conversations with other people, the more I realised that the Antichrists were already here and are working hard to mislead many Christians away from the true gospel of Jesus. Even though many people have the Bible with them, they still don't understand it. So my mission is to reach as many souls as I can before the return of Jesus.

My prayer is that many people's eyes may be opened and the true gospel of Jesus might be known. I grew up in a religious family, where my grandmother wanted to see us attending church every Sunday. When it came to Sundays, she did not want any excuse. My mother was supportive when I joined the Christian church, but she could not understand then why I had to spend most of my time there. One day she agued with me about the time I spent in the church and I tried explaining to her about what the intimate relationship with God was, but she couldn't understand what I was talking about. Then, I made it my mission to pray that God must open her eyes and bring her to a church that was preaching the true gospel of Jesus in full.

Today, as I am writing this book, she is a re-born woman of God, who knows Christ and cannot stay quiet about Him. I have learnt a lot from my mother and my granny concerning good living. They taught me that I should love and respect other people and help those who are in need at a young age. But they did not know at all what was to have an intimate relationship with God then. This made me realise that many good people of God are out there, thinking that doing good to others and attending the church on Sundays makes them Christians and that their destiny will be heaven. They are not taught about having an intimate relationship with their Maker through faith, and what God's plan is for their lives. They are also not taught about the schemes of Satan, so they can always be watchful and involve themselves more in prayer. It is very important to always be alert, because Satan does not have rest. I was caught up in that kind of religion as I was growing up and I know many people are still in the same situation as I was. May prayer is that God may open many people's eyes and they can be saved in Jesus Christ's name.

Scripture quotations are from the New International Version (NIV).

Contents

CHAPTER ONE

  1. The Creation of Man   1
  2. The fall of man   3
  3. Who is Satan?   5

CHAPTER TWO

  1. What is the purpose of the law?   8
  2. Example of the law   11
  3. Do you think God is unfair?   13

CHAPTER THREE

  1. What is faith?   16
  2. Why is Christianity so important?   19
  3. What does it mean to be a Christian?   21
  4. What is it to be born of God?   24
  5. True Christianity   26
  6. Why do we have so many churches?   28

CHAPTER FOUR

  1. Are all people God's children?   32
  2. What is the behaviour of a child of God?   33
  3. Our Christian Journey   37

CHAPTER FIVE

  1. Our final destination   40

i) Hell and the lake of fire   40

ii) Heaven or paradise   43

About the Author   45

CHAPTER ONE

1. The Creation of Man

Genesis 2:1–25 Thus the heavens and the earth were completed in all their vast array. By the seventh day God had finished the work he had been doing; so on the seventh day he rested from all his work. And God blessed the seventh day and made it holy, because on it he rested from all the work of creating that he had done. This is the account of the heavens and the earth when they were created. When the Lord God made the earth and the heavens, and no shrub of the field had yet appeared on the earth and no plant of the field had yet sprung up, for the Lord God had not sent rain on the earth and there was no man to work the ground, but streams came up from the earth and watered the whole surface of the ground, the Lord God formed the man from the dust of the ground and breathed into his nostrils the breath of life, and the man became a living being...)

God created heaven and earth and everything that exists in it. The Bible says that God spoke the word and everything that did not exist came to existence. When man was created, there was a meeting held on how he was to be created. We see that in the bible where it was decide on how he was to be created, which was to be in the image and the likeness of God, and to rule over the earth and every living thing under the heavens.

(Genesis 1:26 Then God said," Let us make man in our image, in our likeness, and let them rule...)

So, man was created to be like God because he was given authority over the entire earth except for one thing. That was the divine plan of God for man to rule over everything and never to suffer. He was created to enjoy a blessed life. God's only expectation from man was to honour and respect Him. Man was given free will to make his own choices. He was placed in a garden called Eden, where there were all kinds of trees pleasing to the eye. In the middle of the garden God placed the tree of life, which was the tree of knowledge of good and evil. Then man was there to work and take good care of it. God commanded man to freely eat from any tree except the one in the middle. He said if man eats from it, he would surely die.

Then the Lord created Eve for Adam, after seeing how lonely Adam was, in spite of all he had. By placing the tree in the garden, God was placing a symbol of obedience, to remind man of His command. I believe that God wanted to make a clear point to them that He's the highest authority over them, even though He gave them authority over other things. Man did not have to work for anything, and he was given control over all things, his duty was just to give God the honour and the glory He deserved. He did not have to pray for any blessings like health, finances or family; he already had it all. It means that he was blessed in all areas of his life and in return he needed to show appreciation by honouring God. Man was not forced to obey, but he had to do that by his own free will.

2. The fall of man

Genesis 3:1–24 Now the serpent was more crafty than any of the wild animals the Lord God had made. He said to the woman," Did God really say, 'You must not eat from any tree in the garden'?" The woman said to the serpent, "We may eat fruit from the trees in the garden, but God did say, 'You must not eat fruit from the tree that is in the middle of the garden, and you must not touch it, or you will die." You will not surely die," the serpent said to the woman. "For God knows that when you eat of it your eyes will be opened, and you will be like God, knowing good and evil." When the woman saw that the fruit of the tree was good for food and pleasing to the eye, and also desirable for gaining wisdom, she took some and ate it. She also gave some to her husband, who was with her, and he ate it. Then the eyes of both of them were opened, and they sewed fig leaves together and made covering for themselves..........)

When we read the story of the fall of man, we ask ourselves why God placed the tree in the middle, knowing that Satan would tempt his people. Even though He knew how evil was Satan and, why did He allow it to happen to His beloved people? Do you think that it was fair of God to do that? God is not unfair, because the Bible tells us that man was created in His image and likeness, so he was like God in most ways. He had God's character, and above all, God was there to guide him. Satan did not come once to tempt Eve but several times, until she became weak to resist. Eve started to waver between God's command and Satan's offer. She knew God as their creator before Satan appeared to her with his proposal, so she had enough motive to trust God, not Satan.

When she felt weak, she had to turn to God for guidance and to tell Him about the proposal of Satan before considering it. She knew that God loved them as a father, and He had their best interest at heart. After all, God created them and everything in the garden was placed under their control, how could He deceive them? They lacked nothing, and God had already blessed them with wisdom to know which trees are good for food and which not. They also had the intelligence to give names to the animals, so they did not need to gain more knowledge of good and evil. Because of doubt, man was tempted and fell into sin.

When God appeared to them, they hid themselves, and He asked them why they hid. They said they were naked and felt ashamed. What they felt was spiritually nakedness because of their disobedience. When confronted by God, instead of man taking responsibility, he shifted the blame to the woman, saying: 'The woman you put here with me gave me the fruit to eat, and I ate.' So Adam shifted the blame to God and the woman. In other words, Adam was just saying to God that if He had not placed the woman there with him, he wouldn't have eaten the fruit. He was just a victim of circumstance. Then God asked the woman, and she shifted the blame to the serpent. She also did not take responsibility for her actions, so she was just also victim as Adam was. God as the father did not kill them but punished them for their mistakes.

Who knows how the story might have turned should they have acknowledged, taken responsibility for and repented from their sins. Maybe God would have given them a chance to continue living in the garden, with perhaps a lighter punishment, and then gotten rid of Satan. God's mercy is upon those who take responsibility for their mistakes and repent of it. The blood of Jesus is always sufficient to wash away all their sins and give them another chance to be saved. So do you think God is unfair?

3. Who is Satan?

Satan is a principal or a chief demon. He used to be an angel of light called Lucifer in heaven, where he lived together with God and the other angels, and they had a good relationship. He later on grew proud, believing that he could be like God. Perhaps, God told the angels His plan of creating man and giving him authority over the earth, so Satan might have been displeased with that. I also believe that He might have told them that, they were going to serve man and take care of him *(Psalms 91:11: For he will command his angels concerning you to guard you in all your ways)*. Out of anger, Satan became very jealousy and did not like that idea at all. He got the other group of angels to rebel against God; they lost the battle; then God chased them out of His kingdom to earth *(Revelation 12:7–9: And there was war in heaven. Michael and his angels fought against the dragon, and the dragon and his angels fought back. But he was not strong enough, and they lost their place in heaven. The great dragon was hurled down—that ancient serpent called the devil, or Satan, who leads the whole world astray. He was hurled to the earth and his angels with him)*. We call them demons or evil spirits today.

So Satan made it his mission to destroy the people of God and cause them to be disobedient, just to pay revenge to God *(Revelation 12:12: But woe to the earth and the sea, because the devil has gone down to you! He is filled with fury, because he knows that his time is short)*. He wanted to get back at God by causing him grief and make sure that the relationship between God and His people is completely destroyed. God created hell as punishment for Satan and his demons. So Satan wants to take as many souls as he can with him. He is very patient and won't rest until everyone is destroyed *(John 10:10: The thief comes only to steal and kill and destroy)*.

Accepting the Lord Jesus as our personal Savoir can defeat him. When one becomes a Christian, he automatically becomes an enemy of the devil, and the never-ending war starts. If the life of a Christian was hard before, it becomes even harder. Why? Because Satan is more concerned about that person's relationship with God *(Mark 4:15: As soon as they hear it, Satan comes and takes away the word that was sown in them)*. Now that the person has left Satan's camp to God's protection,

Satan makes it very hard for that person to be a Christian. He brings lots of obstacles like temptation, doubts, emotions, fears and other things. It is very important for a Christian to have a stable mind, not a doubtful one. Satan is very devoted in seeing Christians losing their faith. He might use family, close friends and anyone else to fight or hate you for no reason.

Christians must seek the Holy Spirit to live inside them for protection and guidance. God always makes a way for His children to overcome Satan's schemes. He comes and puts temptation before us, and we must always be strong to resist him. We can only be strong to resist when we are close to God. We must remember that Satan is spirit and we are flesh, so we need God, as He is spirit to help us overcome him *(John 4:24: God is spirit)*. Also, we need to bear in mind that Satan needs a body to get to us. When dealing with people used by Satan, we must not take it personally and hate those people. We have to destroy the root of the problem, which is spiritual. Some people are just victims of Satan without knowing. We need to pray God to open their eyes, so Satan may lose both souls. If we do not give in to the temptations of the devil, we'll see that he will not have power over us *(James 4:7: Submit yourselves, then, to God. Resist the devil, and he will flee from you)*.

Satan gets the power from us when we give in to his tricks. The Bible says that Satan is roaring like a lion, but he is not a real lion if we become firm in our faith *(1 Peter 5:8: Be self-controlled and alert. Your enemy the devil prowls around like a lion looking for someone to devour)*. He will always try to scare us and wants us to give up our faith in God. We must always stand firm in our faith by being close to God every day.

CHAPTER TWO

1. What is the purpose of the law?

Galatians 3:19–25 What then, was the purpose of the law? It was added because of transgressions until the seed to whom the promise referred had come. The law was put into effect through angels by a mediator. A mediator, however, does not represent just one party; but God is one. Is the law, therefore, opposed to the promises of God? Absolutely not! For if a law had been given that could impart life, then righteousness would certainly have come by the law. But the scripture declares that the whole world is a prisoner of sin, so that what was promised, being given through faith in Jesus Christ, might be given to those who believe. Before this faith came, we were held prisoners by the law, locked up until faith should be revealed. So the law was put in charge to lead us to Christ that we might be justified by faith. Now that faith has come, we are no longer under the supervision of the law.

We know that in the beginning man was placed in the garden where everything was given to him and he lacked nothing. So man didn't have to pray God for any of blessings, because he was fully blessed. God was walking in the garden with him, to give them guidance. He was given free will and he needed to be reminded that God was still his highest authority. So God invented the first law, which was that he was not to touch nor eat from the middle tree. Man had only one law to obey then. God wanted man to show submission and obedience to Him. It was not difficult to obey, for man had everything else to eat from. He just had to give God the honour and the glory He deserved by being obedient.

After man became disobedient to God, he was chased out of the garden, because he was exposed to evil. They had to leave the garden of perfection because they were no longer perfect. As man was growing in numbers, evil was also growing. In Noah's time, God tried to speak through Noah to save his people, but they were caught up in their evil deeds and did not listen to Him. They were abusing their free will and did not give reverence to their creator anymore. So God whipped the earth and started the new generation through Noah and his family *(Genesis 9:1–4: Then God blessed Noah and his sons, saying to them, "Be fruitful and increase in number and fill the earth. The fear and dread of you will fall upon all the beasts of the earth and all the birds of the air, upon every creature that moves along the ground, and upon all the fish of the sea; they are given into your hands. Everything that lives and moves will be food for you. Just as I gave you the green plants, I now give you everything. But you must not eat meat that has its lifeblood still in it")*.

In the times of Moses He showed the children of Israel his love and mercy by delivering them from slavery. Yet they continued to do what was evil. So God came with the law to discipline, never to punish them. God wanted to protect them, for He knew that without the law in place, they would continue living in sin and at the end be destroyed.

Everyone has freedom of choice and Satan is taking advantage of that by misleading people to do the wrong things. People get caught up in Satan's schemes without knowing that they are sinning against God. The law makes it very clear to man what's wrong and what's right. For there will be consequences for breaking the law. God's plan is to live forever with His children in His kingdom *(Hebrews 11:40: God had planned something better for us so that only together with us would they be made perfect)*. The responsibility of being free is to be obedient and respectful and to give honour to our creator. We must always bear in mind that without our creator there is no salvation. Godly respect and love is the key to a very good and successful life on earth. Even though it gets hard to live this good life because of sin, one needs to work harder to make it. We must always turn to our master for guidance in order to keep on doing what He expects from us. Satan will always be the opposing force against those who have reverence to the Lord. We must remember that he does not want to see children of God inheriting eternal life. He will make it very difficult for them to have a peaceful life on earth. We need to remember to run to God all the time, for He is always available to assist us in overcoming Satan.

Because man is imperfect and exposed to sin, God came up with a plan to help man to reach the living standard that will be acceptable to Him. So the law is very important to us children of God. It gives our lives direction *(Matthew 5:17: Do not think that I have come to abolish the Law or Prophets; I have not come to abolish them but to fulfil them)*. When we follow the law of God, it means we respect and obey Him. The law is the second chance that God is giving his children to enter heaven. Without the law we will be lost in our evil deeds unknowingly. The law is the guidance of God and the Bible is the book of the law. It is there to teach us how to live and it is our daily guide. We all know that man was given free will and Satan is determined to keep man astray. He wants man to lose eternity by confusing him. When we have the law, we know what is wrong and what is right. The law was never invented to punish us but to help us. A house or a company without the law will have corruption and confusion because there will be no direction *(Matthew 5:19—20: Anyone who breaks one of the least of this commandments and teaches others to do the same will be called least in the kingdom of heaven, but whoever practises and teaches these commands will be called great in the kingdom of heaven. For*

I tell you that unless your righteousness surpasses that of the Pharisees and the teachers of the law, you will certainly not enter the kingdom of heaven).

Everyone will do what he or she wants and when it suits him or her, and some might commit wrong things without knowledge. It is of the utmost importance to have that law in everything, because it gives direction. Where there is the law there is also the punishment of breaking it. That's why we have heaven and hell at the end of time. The choice we make today, will determine our destiny tomorrow. We must always remember to consult God when we are confused. Be blessed by making the right choice.

2. Example of the law

Matthew 19:19: "I tell you that anyone who divorces his wife, except for marital unfaithfulness, and marries another woman commits adultery."

I believe that Jesus was looking at the intention of divorce, which is the motive behind it. If a partner divorces his partner intending to marry someone else, it is a sin of adultery. He might no longer be satisfied with his partner because he is interested in someone else. So, what God has blessed him with, is no longer appealing to his eyes. Satan is always there to cause destruction and lust, to destroy the union among the couples. He always comes with temptations to destroy the relationship. The partner might start complaining or seeing mistakes in the other partner because his intention is to get out of the marriage. He just wants to break free so that he can be with the other person. It's all about the evil intention of making the other partner feel guilty, thinking that she might have done something wrong to cause this, even though that partner may know that she is not at fault. God's intention is for the couple to be united until death or the return of Jesus. I do not believe that the divorcee is prohibited from finding happiness again. If a person has been divorced and she still wants to get married, I believe God would allow her to do so. I do not believe she would be at fault because it is not she who initiated the divorce, so she is just the victim. God wanted to discipline people and His intention is to keep couples together *(Hebrews 12:5-6: My son, do not make light of the Lord's discipline, and do not lose heart when he rebukes you, because the Lord disciplines those whom he loves, and punishes everyone he accepts as a son).*

But Satan hates unity and he will do anything to destroy that. If there was no direction given to man, what kind of the world we would be living in today? Man will be getting in and out of marriage, breaking people's heart without any concern about the other person's feelings. We will be living in a confused world that will lead many to bloodshed, and Satan knows that. It will be like, If a man sees a woman today and he marries her because of lust and then later Satan bring someone else, he starts desiring that other one and quickly divorces his partner to be with her, and so on and on with the other people also. Discipline was needed to give us order and to keep us safe.

3. Do you think God is unfair?

Malachi 1:2-3: "I have loved you," says the Lord. But you ask, "How have you loved us?" "Was not Esau Jacob's brother?" the Lord says. "Yet I have loved Jacob, but Esau I have hated, and I have turned his mountains into a wasteland and left his inheritance to the desert jackals."

In the book of Malachi, God said, "Jacob I loved and Esau

I hated." This verse really disturbed me so much because I couldn't understand how God could hate someone. If you are hated by God, there's nothing that will be right in your life, because He is the creator of everything. I said that God was unfair for bringing this poor soul on earth just to suffer.

As I continued reading and being concerned, I came to this revelation that Esau never gave value to the things of God, even though he was born in a religious family. He was born in a family that valued God and had a very close relationship with Him. He just did not care much and his attitude was not pleasing to God. He did not hate him personally but hated his attitude. Esau took lightly the things of God to the point that he sold his birthright to fill up his stomach *(Genesis 25:31–33: Jacob replied: "First sell me your birthright." "Look, I am about to die," Esau said. "What good is the birthright to me?" But Jacob said, "Swear to me first." So he swore an oath to him, selling his birthright to Jacob)*. God wanted him to have the treasure of growing His word to the next generations, and he just wanted something that could not even last a day. Esau did not have the vision of God and didn't bother to know it.

Our attitude determines who we are. Jacob his brother always fought to be the best and have a great relationship with God. He always wanted to have a special place in the eyes of God and to be noticed by Him. When the relationship with God is strong, nothing will put you down or make you doubt. If you treat God as your father or best friend, you will always trust Him to be there when you need Him. You do not accept failure or defeat, for you know that your God can do all things. You will fight and never give up, for you know that you have God on your side and He will help you to achieve your dream. You also believe that your victories will give God the glory, so that is why Jacob was a fighter and never accepted a life of defeat *(Genesis 32:26–28: Then the man said, "Let me go, for it is daybreak." But Jacob replied, "I will not let you go unless you bless me." The man asked him, "What is your name?" "Jacob," he answered. Then the man said, "Your name will no longer be Jacob, but Israel, because you have struggled with God and with men and have overcome").*

I believe that after Esau had sold his blessings, he could had gone to God to ask forgiveness and He would have forgiven him, instead of running after his brother and living with resentment most of his life. Repentance is very important for our salvation. What he did well was to forgive his brother, which was a great opportunity to ask God's forgiveness and start over with both God and his brother *(Genesis 33:4: But Esau ran to meet Jacob and embraced him; he threw his arms around his neck and kissed him. And they wept).* God is looking for sincere hearts that will ask forgiveness and repent from their mistakes, and He will give them another chance to be saved. God is a God of many more second chances *(Matthew 18:21-22: Then Peter came to Jesus and asked, "Lord, how many times shall I forgive my brother when he sins against me? Up to seven times?" Jesus answered, "I tell you, not seven times, but seventy-seven times.)*

My son also raised a question one day to me, saying, why did God send Judas to hell while it was His purpose for him to betray Jesus? It is when the Holy Spirit revealed that it was God's plan, but Judas's choice for hell. He had so many chances to repent after he betrayed Jesus, but he didn't use them. He allowed Satan to accuse him and committed suicide. God's purpose was just for Judas to betray Jesus only and not for him to go to hell. I believe that he was greedy and corrupted by the love of money. It was easy for him to sell Jesus for money because he saw an opportunity to make more money quickly. God did not sentence him to destruction, but he did that by himself. Look at Peter; he denied Jesus and felt guilty and repented. He never allowed the guilt to destroy him. That is why he was given a second chance to continue being Christ's disciple. Today we read about Peter being the strongest disciple of Jesus. We can learn from him that no one is perfect, even though we might commit some mistakes. When we acknowledge them and repent, God is able to forgive us and take us back to His presence and bless us.

CHAPTER THREE

1. What is faith?

Faith is more than a feeling but a confirmation of something that has not come to pass yet. Faith is more like trust; it is one with it. When one has faith in something, it is when you determine that something exists or is done without having the evidence of its existence. It is when you are very sure of something by having the assurance inside of your heart *(Hebrews 11:1 Now faith is being sure of what we hope for and certain of what we do not see)*. You do not need to first see or feel that thing before you believe *(2 Corinthians 5:7 We live by faith, not by sight)*. When you hope or dream to have something, then faith comes and gives you the assurance of that thing before it can materialise *(Matthew 11:22–23: "Have faith in God," Jesus answered. "I tell you the truth, if anyone says to this mountain, 'Go. Throw yourself into the sea,' and does not doubt in his heart but believes that what he says will happen, it will be done for him")*.

You must first have faith that gives you trust to be sure that whatever you ask from God, He has already done it before it can physically appear. When you have faith in God, it means that you are sure that He is there even without seeing him with your naked eye *(Hebrews 11:6: And without faith it is impossible to please God, because anyone who comes to Him must believe that He exists and that He rewards those who earnestly seek Him)*. You have to believe that He is bigger and greater than anything that exists. You must trust that he made everything that exists and nothing that exists today is beyond Him. When we believe that He created heaven and earth and they are not bigger than He is, we will understand that He is not limited by the universe we live in, but the universe is just one of His creations. We will not doubt that He is present at any given time, at any place and is powerful and can see us at the same time.

Faith makes us trust that God is king and he has his own kingdom in heaven. His dwelling is bigger and better, more beautiful than the universe we live in. Faith makes us enter the kingdom of God spiritually by revealing to us about our great God and His plans for us *(Romans 1:17: For in the gospel a righteousness from God is revealed, a righteousness that is by faith from first to last, just as it is written: "The righteous will live by faith")*. Faith gives us a clear understanding of what is going on in the heavenly realm. We can clearly identify the works of the evil spirit and the work of God in this world. Faith is what is required to be a servant of God. It is by supernatural faith that we are chosen by God to become his children. Faith gives us confidence in what we believe and it produces power in us. We get more powerful when we have Faith, even in bad situations, faith gives us the assurance that we will pull through. Faith is the key to our salvation. We cannot have salvation without faith and cannot receive blessings from God without it either *(Matthew 9:29–30: Then he touched their eyes and said, "According to your faith will it be done to you," and their sight was restored)*. **Before we pray we must first have faith, and then go on our knees believing that whatever we ask from God, it will be given to us before it materialises. We need to believe that He is mighty and great to give us whatever our request may be. We do not see God with our naked eye, but we see Him spiritually because Faith takes us to the spiritual world. With faith everything is possible. It takes us to the impossible world and makes the impossible happen.**

We must also bear in mind that it takes faith to believe in the evil one and do the evil things, which is why people are succeeding in doing what is evil. They put their entire faith in whatever they do and believe in the results they are going to receive. That is why God doesn't allow His children to be double-minded. He doesn't want to be shared with the devil. When a person is doubtful, he is double-minded, which is the opposite of Faith. He believes in God and at the same time he gives an ear to Satan's voice and becomes doubtful of God's power. Doubt is a strong enemy of faith and is a strong tool of Satan. He uses doubt to rob the children of God of their blessings. He knows that God hates doubts and he continuously uses this doubt to confuse them. Fear make a person think the worst of the situation and start to commit sin after sin, then Faith make him think of the best results. We must always remember what God said in the Holy Scripture about doubts. He said we must never think that we can receive anything from Him by doubting. If we doubt God, we are undermining His power to help us and we are putting limitation on Him. We are actually saying that He is too weak to help us. We are making our God to be a liar by distrusting His capability to bless us. Faith is the key to a life with God here on earth and also in heaven. If you say you love God and believe in him as your Savoir, there must not be any room for doubts in your heart. Challenges in our lives make our faith unstable, but we must always fight to keep it stable. Faith believes beyond what we see, and it brings the future to the present.

2. Why is Christianity so important?

We all know that God created people or human beings, so we are all people of God *(Genesis 1:26: Then God said, "Let us make man in our image, in our likeness, and let them rule over the fish of the sea and the birds of the air, over the livestock, over all the earth, and over all the creatures that move along the ground")*. The Bible tells us how man fell in to sin and how God tried to redeem man from sin by using the kings and prophets in the Bible *(Genesis 3:1–24 now the serpent was more crafty…)*. There we read about the final solution for God to save human beings from eternal punishment by sending His only Son, Jesus Christ, to sacrifice His life for us *(Matthew 1:21: She will give birth to a son, and you are to give him the name Jesus, because he will save his people from their sins. Ephesians 5:2: and live a life of love, just as Christ loved us and gave himself up for us as a fragrant offering and sacrifice to God)*. Jesus volunteered his life by shedding His blood on the cross for us by agreeing to leave His glory in heaven to come here on earth *(Philippians 2:5–7: Your attitude should be the same as that of Christ Jesus: Who, being in very nature God, did not consider equality with God something to be grasped, but made himself nothing, taking the very nature of a servant, being made in human likeness)*. He knew that it was going to be hard but still went through with it just to bring us back to God. He created a way for us to have eternal life with our creator. Jesus knew that without His sacrifice no one would be saved, so that is why we call him our Savoir.

The Bible says Jesus came to destroy the works of the devil and bring life to its fullness. He wants us to have an abundant life just like in the beginning of creation. Christianity comes from Christ; it means the followers of Christ or to be Christ like. To be a Christian is to walk in the footsteps of Jesus Christ and imitate him *(Ephesians 5:1: Be imitators of God, therefore, as dearly loved children).* We can never inherit the kingdom of God without Christ; He is our only key to eternal life. So that is why we need to be born again and become true Christians, in order for us to see the kingdom of God. Satan is telling people that God is love and there is nothing like hell for the unbelievers and are deceived by him. So they believe that all people are God's and they will end up in heaven. As we all know that God exists through the Bible, we should know that the Bible teaches the truth. We cannot choose to believe in some chapters and choose not to believe in others. We read one Bible that clearly tells us that there are two destinations, which are hell and the lake of fire, and heaven and paradise *(Revelation 21:8: But the cowardly, the unbelieving, the vile, the murderers, the sexually immoral, those who practise magic arts, the idolaters and all liars—their place will be in the fiery lake of burning sulphur. This is the second death).* We all have choices to make in order to choose our destiny. I rather believe in what the Bible tells me, unlike not believing at all and finding out after death that hell does exist. For it will be too late for me to turn back and try to fix things. If I believe in the Bible and do what is right and find out that hell does not exist, I would still lose nothing. Why do people need to become Christians? It is to inherit the kingdom of God at the end of time, because there is no other way without Jesus Christ. The Bible warns us about the Antichrist, so that means not all who call themselves Christian are indeed the true Christians or followers of Christ. We will know the tree by its fruits, so watch and pray, as Jesus has warned us.

3. What does it mean to be a Christian?

We all know that Jesus Christ left his throne to come down to earth to set mankind free from the captivity of sin. All people were under the control of the evil one and Christ offered to sacrifice himself as a sacrificial offering for our sins. Christ asked Father God to come down to earth to sacrifice His own life in order for us to have a chance for eternity with our God in heaven. He came here on earth in an earthly suit *(Hebrews 2:14: Since the children have flesh and blood, he too shared in their humanity…)*. Jesus had all the emotions a human being has *(John 11:38: Jesus, once more deeply moved, came to the tomb)* Satan tempted Him also, but He never gave in to his temptation *(Matthew 4:1–11 Then Jesus was led by the Spirit into the desert to be tempted by the devil. After fasting forty days and forty nights, he was hungry. The temper came to him and said, "If you are the Son of God, tell these stones to become bread." Jesus answered," It is written: 'Man does not live on bread alone, but on every word that comes from the mouth of God." Then the devil took him to the holy city and made him stand on the highest point of the temple. "Throw yourself down. For it is written: ' He will command his angels concerning you, and they will lift you up in their hands, so that you will not strike your foot against a stone." Jesus answered him, "It is written: 'Do not put the Lord your God to the test." …)*. He endured all that humiliation because of the love he had for us. He came to show us how to overcome the world by overcoming sin everyday. To be a Christian is to imitate Christ, by living as an overcomer just like our Savoir did. Jesus was always praying and keeping a close relationship with God. *(Luke 18:1: Then Jesus told his disciples a parable to show them that they should always pray and not give up. Also see Luke 22:40.)* By keeping a close relationship with God; it helped Him to overcome Satan. We as

Christians, we also need to have a close relationship with God by His Spirit so we can overcome Satan just like Jesus.

When a person accepts Jesus as his personal Savoir and becomes a Christian, Satan becomes very angry and starts to wage war against that person. He makes the person's life difficult by making sure that he experiences difficulties in areas he never did before *(Revelation 12:17: Then the dragon was enraged at the woman and went off to make war against the rest of her offspring—those who obey God's commandments and hold to the testimony of Jesus)*. Satan wants the person to give up and start blaming God for the problems he's experiencing. He sends more of his demons to cause destruction in the person's life. He might even cause confusion among the family members. When a person becomes a Christian, he must bear in mind that he's engaging himself into an everlasting warfare with the devil. We must also remember that Satan is very patient and will not give up until we are destroyed. We must always have a close relationship with God in order to defeat him because we need the help of the Holy Spirit. We need to place our faith in the right place, which is in God, not on other things. With God on our side we are sure of our victory, because God is spirit, and so is Satan. We need to have the Spirit of God in order to defeat Satan. Satan is more worried about the true Christians because he does not want anyone to be saved; he only wants to see people going to hell with him.

\

Jesus came to destroy the devil's work and He can only accomplish that if we are willing to become His children in truth and in spirit. God wants all his people to be saved through His son Jesus. We must remember that when Jesus was tempted, He never gave in to temptations. He defeated the devil by referring him to the word, saying that "It is written". It shows how important to know the scriptures, because you can always refer back to them. He became angry when he saw people turning the church into a business place, selling and buying things there. Jesus threw their things away and disciplined them *(Matthew 21:12: Jesus entered the temple area and drove out all those who were buying and selling there. He overturned the tables of the money changers and the benches of those selling doves...)*. He never held any grudge against anyone, but acted on His anger by disciplining them, and got over it immediately. Apostle Paul said: "In your anger do not sin."*(Ephesians 4:26: "In your anger do not sin" Do not let the sun go down while you are still angry)* Jesus was very humble even though being God; he still remained humble here on earth. Jesus's character is what we should have as His followers. So, this is just an example of how human Jesus was and gave us example on how to live as children of God. We need to learn to forgive in painful situations and learn to love and pray for those who hate us. We can learn all this through the Spirit of God.

By becoming a Christian, it does not mean we will have an easy life, but it means we will face challenges and obstacles and eventually we will get through them. We must hold on for we know we have a goal to achieve *(Philippians 3:12–14: Not that I have already obtained all this, or have already been made perfect, but I press on to take hold of that for which Christ Jesus took hold of me. Brothers, I do not consider myself yet to have taken hold of it. But one thing I do: Forgetting what is behind and straining towards what is ahead, I press on towards the goal to win the prize for which God has called me...)*. When Satan fights harder, we must put more effort to fight even more, for we know our God is an overcomer, and so are we. Jesus said we must carry our cross and follow Him; which means it will not be easy, for there will be lots of challenges and tribulations, but we must fight to overcome them all *(Luke 9:23: Then he said to them all: "If anyone would come after me, he must deny himself and take up his cross daily and follow me").* As Jesus was carrying His cross he was falling down and He never stayed down there; He was looking at overcoming His goal, which was the cross to free us. That is the example we need to follow as we are going through the hard moments in our lives. We must just focus on our goal, which is heaven.

4. What is it to be born of God?

When a person becomes a Christian it is very important for the person to be baptised in water and the Holy Spirit. To be baptised in water means that a person goes in the water as a sinner and buries his sinful nature, then comes out as a new person. He kills the old life and leaves it in the past, then starts a new one with God. This act takes place spiritually by faith. It does not mean that when you deep yourself in water you automatically come out as a new person. One needs to have the determination to bury the old self and be willing to fight a day-to-day war to keep his old self buried forever. The Holy Spirit enables us to do that, which is why we need Him in our daily lives. The Bible tells us that when the Holy Spirit comes, we will have power *(Acts 1:8: But you will receive power when the Holy Spirit comes on you).* We need to seek the Holy Spirit daily and invite Him to come and baptise us. The Spirit of God will never come into a life full of sins. We need to empty ourselves from all the sins and invite Him to occupy the empty space in our life.

When we receive the Holy Spirit, the battle becomes easier. We can talk to God any time at any place, even in our hearts. The Holy Spirit is God in us *(John 14:17: the Spirit of truth. The world cannot accept him, because it neither sees him nor knows him. But you know him, for he lives with you and will be in you).* He is there to talk, guide and protect us at all times.

The battle against our own flesh becomes a bit easier when we have Him to help.

The Bible says that those who are born of God overcome the world and their own faith *(1John 5:4: for everyone born of God overcomes the world. This is the victory that has overcome the world, even our faith)*. It means that our faith does not remain constant all the time but wavers. Sometimes you find yourself faced with lots of challenges that make your faith weak but the Spirit of God sustains it again. So it is very true when the Bible says that we are able to overcome our faith. When you're faced with a battle you do not face it alone. God is there to face it with you, and then you overcome because your helper is there to see you through.

To be born of God means that we have to seek the Holy Spirit and ask Him to come inside of us. We must continuously ask Him to remain in us and help us to grow strong in Him day by day *(John 15:7: If you remain in me and my words remain in you...)*. We as children of God will always be faced with challenges; that is why it's so important for us to keep a very close relationship with God. The disciples of Jesus became very strong after receiving the Holy Spirit and they started to perform great miracles. When our faith is down we have the Spirit of God to pull us through. Even though we might feel down, the love of God inside us sustains us. So the most important fruit of the Spirit is love. We need to ask God to teach us how to love Him and other people. Love is the greatest fruit to have because it produces all other fruits of the Spirit.

5. True Christianity

True Christians are those who follow the teachings of Jesus in the Bible fully. They do not select what suits them and chose to follow only that, or even twist the scripture to suit their needs. But they obey the word of God in full and seek His presence daily. They are those whose faith is only in God. Christians need to have a very close relationship with God at all times. A true Christian does not become a Christian only on Sundays when he goes to the church, but will always seek God's guidance every day. To be a Christian one needs to first hear the word of God, accept it, and then confess with his own mouth that Jesus Christ is the Lord and Savoir of his life, then be baptised in water *(Matthew 3:11: "I baptise you with water for repentance...").* To be baptised in water means you are killing the old sinful nature and being born again to a new person who is changed and wants to please God. Then, this Christian is to seek the Holy Spirit who baptised him and make a new home inside his heart.

It is very important for a true Christian to have the Holy Spirit because without the Holy Spirit the Christian is not born of God. The Bible says that the true worshippers are those who worship God in truth and in spirit *(John 4:24: God is spirit, and his worshippers must worship in spirit and in truth).* Jesus' disciple needed the Holy Spirit before going into the world to do the work of God. Jesus himself needed the baptism of water and the Holy Spirit to do the miracles he did. We see that when John the Baptist baptised Jesus, the Bible says the Holy Spirit came like a dove on Jesus *(Matthew 3:16: As soon as Jesus was baptised, he went up out of the water. At that moment heaven was opened, and he saw the spirit of God descending like a dove and lighting on him).* Christians without the Holy Spirit are like the believers who do not have the foundation of God in them and anytime they are faced with obstacles or trials, they lose their faith and become discouraged from continuing their journey. But those who are born of God have greater power inside them that enables them to carry on and gives them hope.

The Holy Spirit is God in us; He always guides, protects moulds, strengthens, encourages, and speaks to us all the time. To have God living inside of us we don't need to have a secret place to pray; we can speak to Him anytime, anywhere, as long as we open our hearts in request or in thanksgiving. A Christian needs to seek the Holy Spirit earnestly until he receives Him, even after receiving, he must keep on seeking. God will never come upon someone without the invitation. The Holy Spirit will never come in to someone whose life is full of sins, which means that a person must live a clean life free from sins.

When one receives the Spirit of God, he will recognise the fruits of the Holy Spirit, which are love, joy, peace, patience, kindness, goodness, faithfulness, gentleness and self-control *(Galatians 5:22: But the fruit of the Spirit is love...)*. We must bear in mind that the fruits of the Spirit are the same but the gifts are different. If a person is born of God, he must have the same fruit of God's Spirit *(Matthew 7:16: By their fruit you will recognise them)*. Gifts are different; for example, one can have a gift of healing, wisdom, interpretation of tongues, and the other a gift of prophecy, just like the disciples, who did not have the same gifts.

When a person is born of God, it means he is carrying the Spirit of God inside him. God leaves inside of that person and he does not continue living in sin, but fights to be pure and righteous to please his master *(1 John 3:6: No one who lives in him keeps on sinning. No one who continues to sin has either seen him or known him)*. He never takes decisions without consulting God first. The Bible says that blessed are those who fight for righteousness, for none is righteous because we

26

have fallen short of God's glory. We are in a journey that will take us to our final destination that we choose. Jesus said to his disciples that they must go into the world and preach the gospel so that many people may be saved, so this is what is required to all Christians before the coming of Jesus again. The Gospel should be preached all over the world, and then Jesus can come back and take His church. We as Christians must always bear in mind to watch and pray because the Antichrists are already here on earth to confuse us. Jesus said in Matthew 24 that, in the last days, even the chosen would be deceived. So we really need to open our minds, hearts and eyes and be very careful.

6. Why do we have so many churches?

What is a church? A church is not a building made by bricks, but they call that building a church because of a group of people who gather in that building in one purpose, which is to serve God. A true church is an individual who attends services in that building; he gives the building a name.

We find so many churches in the world under the umbrella of Christianity. I believe that they can be different churches that preach the true Christianity because of the different gifts the founders might have. When a person becomes baptised with the Holy Spirit, he will bear the same fruit of the Spirit of God and God will bless him with gifts, which will be different to those of the other person *(1 Corinthians 12:4–6: There are different kinds of gifts, but the same Spirit. There are different kinds of service, but the same Lord. There are different kinds of working, but the same God works all of them in all men…).* If one is blessed with the gift of healing, his church will excel in that gift because he is the founder of his own church according to his gift. The other person will excel in the gift of prophecy and visions and the other one in other gifts and so on. We must not be jealous of other people's gifts; we must seek God and ask Him to reveal our gift to us, so we can fulfil our purpose accordingly *(1 Corinthians 12:7: Now to each one the manifestation of the spirit is given for the common good).* We must remember that we are unique and can never be someone else, so we must not try to imitate others. What I have witnessed is that one person might have a gift of preaching and the other will try to preach also, thinking that he can also do it or even do it better because he's been in the church more years that the other person. What is that? It is pure evil and God doesn't appreciate that, while his concentrating on others' gifts, he's loosing the opportunity to explore his.

We must remember always that the true church is the one that preaches salvation, and a life of faith. The purpose of the church buildings is where the children of God gathers together and have teachings on how to have communion with God and leader are not afraid to teach people the truth. People need to be taught how to live the correct lives in order to please God and be taught how to inherit eternity with God. They must be taught the truth about the consequences of living a wrongful life *(Galatians 5:19–21 The acts of the sinful nature are obvious: sexual immorality, impurity and debauchery, idolatry and witchcraft, hatred, discord, jealousy, fits of rage, selfish ambition, dissensions, factions and envy; drunkenness, orgies and the like. I warn you, as I did before, that those who live like this will not inherit the kingdom of God).* They need to learn how to have a relationship with God and other people.

The church is where the children of God must come together and be happy. We must stop criticising other fellow Christians because they don't do the same things as we do. We must learn to respect and share our gifts with one another in order to become powerful against the devil and his army. We must stop criticising each other because those who are still in darkness will never desire to come to the light because of our attitude. The true church is the one that follows the teachings of Jesus in full. It makes me very sad when I see the children of God competing with and criticising each other because they're in different congregations forgetting that we as different parts, we complete the body of Christ (1 Corinthians 1:11–12: My brothers, some from Chloe's household have informed me that there are quarrels among you. What I mean is this: One of you says, "I follow Paul"; another, "I follow Apollos"; another…). The body has many parts and each and every part has its special task, and they are all important to form a body. We must learn to come together and unite. Satan becomes very happy when we fight against each other and make our father sad.

The Bible says that there are different kinds of gift and there will also be different kinds of service. We must use our gifts to glorify our God and bless many souls. We must learn to work together and learn from each other, not be jealous. If we concentrate on other people's gifts, we will lose our purpose in life. We need to do what God has brought us here for and stop looking at what other people are doing. We must be the best and be unique in whom we were created to be. Every person is born with a special purpose and if we concentrate on others, then who will complete our purpose? Remember that after everything has passed, God will reward everyone according to his or her deeds. We must portray LOVE to all mankind in spite of their deeds (Ephesians 5:1–2: Be imitators of God, therefore, as dearly loved children and live a life of love, just as Christ loved us and gave himself up for us as a fragrant offering and sacrifice to God).

We need to learn how to help those who have been blinded by the false doctrines and do it wisely if we want to win them back to God. We must always pray for wisdom on how to approach them because they might have strong believes in their doctrine. We must learn to listen and be understanding, try to find out more about their religious background without criticising them, embrace them with love and get to know them as the people of God. We will win their souls to God at the end. Before we judge others, let's remember that we are all God's people and help one another by learning more about one another. By hush judgement, we are pushing them back to Satan, we rather leave the Holy Spirit to do all the talking *(Luke 12:11–12: "When you are brought before synagogues, rulers and authorities, do not worry about how you will defend yourselves or what you will say, for the Holy Spirit will teach you at that time what you should say")*. We can be better people if we walk in LOVE. Jesus, when he was praying for His disciple, said: I pray that they may LOVE each other so that when the world sees them loving one another they will know that they are my disciples *(John 17:6–19: " I have revealed you to those whom you gave me out of the world. They were yours; you gave them to me and they have obeyed your word. Now they know that everything you have given me comes from you.....)*.

That is the request our Master made for us as His children, to love one another. Let's destroy the devil by loving one another in spite of our differences; it will really bring us closer to our creator. True Christianity is based on LOVE for our father is LOVE. Let's stop this jealousy and silly competition against one another and start motivating and encouraging our fellow brothers and sisters in using their gifts, in order to grow the kingdom of God. It all starts with me and continues with you.

CHAPTER FOUR

1. Are all people God's children?

Romans 8:14–17: because those who are led by the Spirit of God are sons of God… and 1 John 3:4–10: Everyone who sins breaks the law; in fact, sin is lawlessness. But you know that he appeared so that he might take way our sins. And in him is no sin. No one who lives in him keeps on sinning. No one who continues to sin has either seen him or known him. Dear children, do not let anyone lead you astray. He who does what is right is righteous, just as he is righteous. He who does what is sinful is of the devil, because the devil has been sinning from the beginning. The reason the Son of God appeared was to destroy the devil's work. No one who is born of God will continue to sin, because God's seed remains in him; he cannot go on sinning because he has been born of God. This is how we know who the children of God are and who the children of the devil are: Anyone who does not do what is right is not a child of God, nor is anyone who does not love his brother.

God is the creator and everything exits because of Him, so it means that everything is the creation of God. Yes, all people are God's people, but not all are God's children. Satan did not create anyone; even he is God's creation. We find people who acknowledge God as their father and dedicate themselves to live for Him. We also find other people who do not want anything to do with God, and they believe in themselves or on other gods of this world. People who disobey God and do not serve Him are not His children, but those who serve Him and obey Him are. The Bible says if we believe in God and receive His Holy Spirit, we become His children.

We must remember that though we are all His people, we only become the heirs of salvation by accepting Christ as our Savior. The Bible also says that those who do evil belong to their father the devil. So it is by choice to be a child of God or of Satan. Satan is destined for hell and children of God are destined for heaven. So it means that those who choose God will follow him to heaven and those who choose Satan will follow him to hell. We must remember that if we do not choose God we automatically choose Satan. There's nothing like a middle position. Our choice determines our future. God bless you all. Remember, we reap what we plant and indeed God is love but He is also just.

2. What is the behaviour of a child of God?

The Bible tells us that if a person is a child of God, he does not continue living a sinful life. He strives to please God by sacrificing his fleshly desires that are contrary to God's law. When a person becomes born of God and used to smoke, sleep around, lie and do all other wrong things, he stops completely and prays for strength to live right in order to please God. If a person had friends who are involved in wrong things and are a bad influence to him, he cuts them off from his life (1 Corinthians 15:33: Do not be misled: Bad company corrupts good character). The Bible clearly tells us that light and darkness have nothing in common. So it also says we must not be yoked together with unbelievers, because we do not have anything in common with them (2 Corinthians 6:14–16: Do not be yoked together with unbelievers. For what do righteousness and wickedness have in common? Or what fellowship can light have with darkness? What harmony is there between Christ and Belial? What does a believer have in common with an unbeliever? What agreement is there between the temple of God and idols? For we are the temple of the living God).

People who don't believe in God think our faith is foolishness; they always criticize us. To avoid the criticism and the traps to make us fall into their non-beliefs, we must avoid being friends with them. It does not mean you don't speak to them or sit in the same room with them; you need to know how to deal with that kind of people. Who knows; you might win them to the Lord by having the right attitude. Never engage yourself in an argument concerning your faith; rather, respect their opinion to avoid noise. Remember that God created every one of us and He gave us freewill and everybody is entitle to his own opinion. We must never force anyone to believe in what we believe and must not resent him or her for not believing in the same things as us. Rather we must pray and ask God to open their eyes *(James 5:20: remember this: Whoever turns a sinner away from the error of his way will save him from death and cover a multitude of sins)*. If we treat them with love and try to understand their point of view, we can easily win them at the end.

One day I came across an ex-colleague of mine who was married to a non-Christian and she grew up as a Christian. She asked me not to criticize her for being from another religion, as other Christians did, and she asked if it was wrong to believe in a different religion. I asked her why she asked me that, and she said that she was confused and not sure if she was doing the right thing. I promised never to criticize her but listen to her explaining her husband's religion to me. I said to her that when I pray I use the name of Jesus as my mediator according to Christianity, and she said she uses the name of their religion's prophet, so I asked her not to use their prophet's name and I will not use Jesus but will pray to God the father only. We made that prayer for a week, being in fast for God to reveal the true religion to her. After a week she told me that she believes that the Bible teaches the true religion as she went through it, and now she believes in Jesus as her only Savior. She turned to

Christianity because of my attitude. *(2 Peter 2:12: Live such good lives among the pagans that, though they accuse you of doing wrong, they may see your good deeds and glorify God on the day he visits us. 1 Timothy 3:7: He must also have a good reputation with outsiders, so that he will not fall into disgrace and into the devil's trap.)* I never judged her, but I respected and listened to her. I was very kind and showed interest to her as a creation of God not passing any judgement.

From that day on I learned so much from the Holy Spirit who was using me and taught me all of that. He taught me how to deal with different people and how to listen to them before I pass judgement and lose souls to the devil. The fruits of the Holy Spirit will only be in control of our lives if we allow Him to be. Many Christians are very quick to pass judgement on other people instead of approaching them with love and educating them. God is love and we must remember to always walk in love and help those who are lost. Our attitude is the one that will determine if we are born of God or not *(Philippians 2:5: Your attitude should be the same as that of Christ Jesus)*.

Those who are born of God also become angry and disappointed. When we are angry we must remember not to commit sins and hold grudges against anyone. In our anger we must always calm down, and try to resolve the problem in a stable mind with the person who angered us. We must not go to the next person and start to spread gossip; instead we must call that person in secret and resolve the matter. If a person is rude and is not willing to listen, go to someone you can trust to help you resolve the matter. It is always good to humble yourself and say "I am sorry" if you are at fault. Even if you are not at fault it also the right thing to do to apologise; you avoid arguments. If a person decides to yell and cause a scene, you keep quiet and avoid him until he's tiered and keeps quiet. Our characters as children of God are very important and we must always try to imitate our Lord Jesus Christ.

Watch out for those people who like to take advantage of Christians' kindness; they always borrow money or things and not return them. Perhaps a person testifies about the blessings God blessed him with, then another people rush to borrow money and other material things from that person. Be alert on those kinds of people; I am not saying that it is wrong to help, but do it wisely. It is not a sin to say no or even to demand what is yours. If a person has borrowed something from you, you have the right to go and ask for payment or to ask it back. Being a Christian is not stupidity, but God has blessed us with the spirit of wisdom and discernment. Above all, watch and pray and allow the Spirit of God to guide you, by keeping a close relationship with God at all times. Children of God are the light of the world and we must always do good to show others how to live as Christians *(Matthew 5:16: In the same way, let your light shine before men, that they may see your good deeds and praise your Father in heaven).* We must remember that we are always watched and Satan will make sure that if we do wrong, we are exposed. We must live a holy life not only in front of your fellow believers, and be positive even in tough situations. It is not easy to be a Christian but we must fight to enter through the narrow gate by living a life of sacrifice *(Matthew 7:13: Enter through the narrow gate. For wide is the gate and broad is the road that leads to destruction, and many enter through it).*

It is good to always be around the other Christians to encourage each other and motivate one another. Always join together in prayers and fasting to help each other in prayers. Come together and study the Bible and share the different gifts among yourselves. Teach your children the way of Christ while they are still young. If you are already married to a non-Christian, pray for him or her to have the encounter with God. If not married yet, look for someone in the same church as you, because the teachings are the same. There are so many things that I wish to say, but I pray more that the Holy Spirit may reveal them to you in your journey. *(1 Corinthians 2:10: but God has revealed it to us by his Spirit). Above all, have the intelligent faith.*

3. Our Christian Journey

Ephesians 6:10–18: Finally, be strong in the Lord and in his mighty power. Put on the full armour of God so that you can take your stand against the devil's schemes. For our struggle is not against flesh and blood, but against the rulers, against the authorities, against the powers of this dark world and against the spiritual forces of evil in the heavenly realms. Therefore put on the full armour of God, so that when the day of evil comes, you may be able to stand your ground, and after you have done everything, to stand. Stand firm then, with the belt of truth buckled around your waist, with the breastplate of righteousness in place, and with your feet fitted with the readiness that comes from the gospel of peace. In addition to all this, take up the shield of faith, with which you can extinguish all the flaming arrows of the evil one. Take the helmet of salvation and the sword of the Spirit, which is the word of God. And pray in the Spirit on all occasions with all kinds of prayers and requests…

Becoming a Christian does not happen overnight; it's a journey that we need to take every day for the rest of our lives. It is not an easy journey because we are in conflict with Satan, his demons and our own self. We are faced with a never-ending battle until we leave this earth to be united with our Savoir Jesus Christ. Paul said that we must put on the full armour of God; he was warning us that a Christian life is not an easy life to live. We need to have the spiritual armour of God, with the belt of truth buckled around our waist and the breastplate of righteousness in place. In addition, we need to take up the shield of faith and the helmet of salvation. When Paul spoke of putting on the full armour of God, he meant that we must prepare to have a never-ending battle with the evil one and to cover ourselves with God. We fight a spiritual battle and we need spiritual power to help us overcome. So we need God's help because He is spirit and so is Satan. As the soldier puts on the full uniform of war, we also must put on the full dress code of war, which is the full armour of God. We must always prepare for war, for Satan is always ready to strike at any time, any minute and any second, to catch us off guard. We must never lose sight and must be ready all the time. To stand our ground is to be ready and on guard for Satan's attacks.

To stand firm with the belt of truth means we must not doubt God in us. We must have the confirmation that Satan is the loser; he lost his place in heaven and he lost his battle with Christ on the cross and he will also lose this battle against us when we believe in that. We must always remind him that he lost and will always be a loser in Jesus' name *(Revelation 12:11: They overcame him by the blood of the Lamb and by the word of their testimony)*. We need to do that in confidence and can only do that with the breastplate of righteousness. It means we need to be born of God and live a clean life before Him. We must not give Satan a chance to accuse us, by doing what is pleasing to him *(Ephesians 4:27: and do not give the devil a foothold)*. So the breastplate is the confidence of living a righteous life before God. We need to get our feet fitted with the readiness that comes from the gospel of peace. We must always be ready to move into the battle, for we already know that the victory is ours because the Bible tells us that if we are born of God we are more than overcomers. We must always believe that God is with us and He will give us victory. To take up the shield of faith, means that we can never be the children of God without faith. We must always believe in God who is willing to save us from Satan and never doubt. By faith we are able to overcome any battles, challenges and temptations we are faced with.

Faith gives us confidence in the victory before it materialises, when we put our trust in our Savior. By faith we have the power to distinguish all the flaming arrows of the devil and are able to stand firm and fight everything that Satan throws at us. Faith means that our battle takes place spiritually first before it can be materialised, and we must first overcome it spiritually by prayer. Taking the helmet of salvation means that we will be standing in victory at the end of everything. We will rejoice having our victory that will be eternity with our God in heaven. The helmet symbolises the victory and the reward that will be given to us for fighting the good fight by the sword of the spirit, which is the word of God *(2 Timothy 4:7: I have fought the good fight, I have finished the race, I have kept the faith. 8 Now there is in store for me the crown of righteousness, which the Lord, the righteous Judge, will award to me on that day)*. At the end of it all, you will spread the gospel by being a testimony and strengthening the weak. Our testimony will be the power to many Christians and it will always remind them of our Christian journey.

CHAPTER FIVE

1. Our final destination

The Bible says that there will only be two destinations, which are hell and the lake of fire, and paradise and heaven

i) Hell and the lake of fire

Hell and the lake of fire were created for Satan and his demons, never for the people of God *(Matthew 25:41: Then he will say to those on his left, "Depart from me, you who are cursed, into the eternal fire prepared for the devil and his angels")*. God wants all His people to go to Him in heaven; unfortunately, it is by choice that we will choose where we want to go *(Galatians 6:8: The one who sows to please his sinful nature, from that nature will reap destruction,)*. Even though it grieves God to see His people choosing hell with Satan, He cannot interfere with our free will. As we all know that here on earth, if you break the law, you will face consequences; if you break God's law, you will pay the price. By not adhering to the rules of Christian living, you automatically choose your destiny with the devil. There is no line in between. You follow either God or Satan. If you refuse to do what Jesus is commanding, even though you attend the church, your destiny will be hell and the lake of fire.

Jesus said many are called but few are chosen *(Matthew 22:14: For many are invited, but few are chosen.)*. He meant that the truth is preached to all those who hear the message, but there are only a few who accept the message and live by it. They are the chosen ones, because they chose to be chosen. God does not have favouritism; He is just because His love is the same for all His people. We are the ones who choose to obey Him or not. He is pleading with us to open our hearts so He can enter and live in us *(Revelation 3:20: Here I am! I stand at the door and knock. If anyone hears my voice and opens the door, I will go in and eat with him, and he with me).* Being a churchgoer and refusing to open your heart to Him is a waste of time. Jesus spoke about those who will say to Him that they were churchgoers or religious people, they were doing this and that—and He will chase them away from Him *(Matthew 7:21–23: Not everyone who says to me, "Lord, Lord," will enter the kingdom of heaven, but only he who does the will of my Father who is in heaven. Many will say to me on that day, "Lord, Lord, did we not prophesy in your name and in your name drive out demons and perform many miracles?" Then I will tell them plainly, "I never knew you. Away from me, you evildoers!').* He will not recognise them, because they won't have the mark of the Holy Spirit in them.

Automatically if you do not choose heaven, then you chose hell. Have you ever imagined what the lake of fire will be like? I have. The Bible says that it is a place of torment, the fiery lake of burning sulphur *(Revelation 19:20: The two of them were thrown alive into the fiery lake of burning sulphur).* It means the fire does not stop and neither becomes weak; but keeps burning forever. So if a person is send to the fiery lake of sulphur, he will be in torment forever. We must not forget that our souls were made to live for eternity. The lake of fire is the second death *(Revelation 20:14: Then death and Hades were thrown into the lake of fire. The lake of fire is the second death).* All you will hear will be screaming voices because the place will be very dark and there will never be light again. Think on how painful it feels when your finger is burned for just a second; how would you explain the pain? Can you stand the pain of putting your finger on a candle fire for a little while longer? I don't think so.

So what about your entire body? It is scary, isn't it? My friend, I am not trying to scare you but simply trying to open your eyes. The lake of fire is no joke but a reality *(Luke 16:23–24: In hell, where he was in torment, he looked up and saw Abraham far away, with Lazarus by his side, so he called to him, "Father Abraham, have pity on me and send Lazarus to dip his tip of his finger in water and cool my tongue, because I am in agony in this fire").*

God wants all of us to avoid it, for it was not meant for us *(Revelation 19:20: But the beast was captured, and with him the false prophet who had performed the miraculous signs on his behalf. With these signs he had deluded those who had received the mark of the beast and worshipped his image).* Do not let anyone or anything leads you to hell, because you will be alone in that torment; they won't share your pain with you. It will be everyone for himself. It is not late yet to choose life. Jesus is still knocking at the door of your heart. Please let Him in today and avoid destruction and torment *(Luke 16:27–29: He answered, "Then I beg you, father, send Lazarus to my father's house, for I have five brothers. Let him warn them, so that they will not also come to this place of torment." Abraham replied, "They have Moses and the Prophets; let them listen to them").*

ii) Heaven or paradise

Everyone wants to go to heaven, and they all think that they will end up there. But that is not true; in fact, they are deceiving themselves. I never heard a person saying that when he dies he will go to hell, never. Satan is lying to the people by telling them that there is no hell, it is just a myth because God will never send anyone to a place of destruction. In fact, hell does not exist, there only heaven. What amazes me is that people are quick to believe in this God that we read about in the Bible and only choose to believe in the good things but never in the bad ones. We also read about hell or the lake of fire in the same Bible.

It's by doing what God expects of us that we enter heaven. The Bible says that we must be holy as our Father is holy. It means that we can only be holy beings when the Holy Spirit comes inside of us. He will make us holy and separated *(1 Peter 1:16: for it is written, "Be holy, because I am holy")*. We also read in the Bible about the multitude from all corners of the earth, standing before Jesus *(Revelation 7:9: After this I looked and there before me was a great multitude that no one could count, from every nation, tribe, people and language, standing before the throne and in front of the Lamb)*. It will be all those who were striving to inherit the kingdom of God and never listened to anyone or allowed anything to lead them astray. They stayed strong in their faith, in spite of the challenges they came across. They were never born perfect, but they washed themselves daily in the blood of Jesus *(Revelation 7:14: These are they who have come out of the great tribulation, they have washed their robes and made them white in the blood of the Lamb)*.

We know that no one is perfect, but Jesus is pouring His spirit upon us as the mark for salvation. The Holy Spirit is there at all times to see to it that our journey doesn't become impossible to overcome. He helps us through our journey until we reach our destiny. The Bible says that in heaven, we will not face hunger, trials, temptations, sickness, darkness and all other evil things that we faced here on earth. We will be united with our heavenly father and angels will take good care of us and we will be happy all the time *(Psalms 91:11: For he will command his angels concerning you to guard you in all your ways, they will lift you up in their hands, so that you will not strike your foot against a stone).* We will worship by singing praises to Him and live together with all the other kings and prophets of the past. We will never have to work for anything ever again, and sin will never be in existence there. It will be far better than the Garden of Eden by far. It seems hard to achieve our goal here on earth, for Satan knows that he will never experience heaven again; that is why he fights so hard that we may not go either. We must press on more and more to overcome him, for we know what is awaits us after all this. Please, people of God, I pray that all of us may choose heaven as our destiny, because when we arrive there, we will forget all about our struggles on earth. Let us choose God today, please *(Revelation 1:8: "I am the Alpha and the Omega," says the Lord God, "Who is, and who was, and who is to come, the Almighty").*

ABOUT THE AUTHOR

Ruth Robaine was born in 1974, in a township called Mamelodi at Pretoria, South Africa. Married to George and have one son called Mpho. At an early age she felt an emptiness in her heart that caused by not having an intermate relationship with God. The great encounter took place in 1994 which brought a great change in her life. From that change she felt a very strong desire to share her experience with others. Her experience and communion with God are her inpiration to write and to lead many souls to the Lord.